I AM NOTHING

THE LIGHT OF EMPTINESS

RAVI BHARDWAJ

DISHA RATHOUR

Contents

CHAPTER ONE

Understanding the darkness

Darkness misunderstood

What if darkness was not a void but a passage?
A threshold, not an end—a space where truth whispers beneath the noise?
Do you run from it or dare to sit within it? To listen—to truly listen—to what it has to say?
Look within. What do you fear will emerge from the silence?

The Shadow You Refuse to Face

Is it the unknown that terrifies you or the truths you already suspect?
We spend lifetimes escaping— filling the void with distractions, noise, and illusions of certainty.
Yet darkness waits, patient and unwavering, holding the parts of you have abandoned.
Will you turn away again, or will you finally meet yourself?

The Weight of Unseen Wounds

How much of your suffering comes not from the darkness itself but from resisting it?
What if pain is not punishment but a messenger?
Can you sit with it, not as a victim, but as a witness?
What would happen if, for once, you stopped fighting the night?

The Doorway Hidden in Shadows

Darkness does not swallow, it reveals.
It strips away the false, the fragile, the borrowed identities.
And in the emptiness, something stirs— a quiet knowing, a flicker of something real.
Maybe the light was never missing. Perhaps it was waiting for you to close your eyes and see.

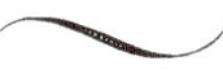

CHAPTER TWO

HEALING FROM DARKNESS

Darkness only heals

Darkness is not an enemy; it is a mirror. It does not swallow—it reveals.
The wounds, the whispers, the selves we abandoned. To heal, we must see. Not escape, not deny—SEE.

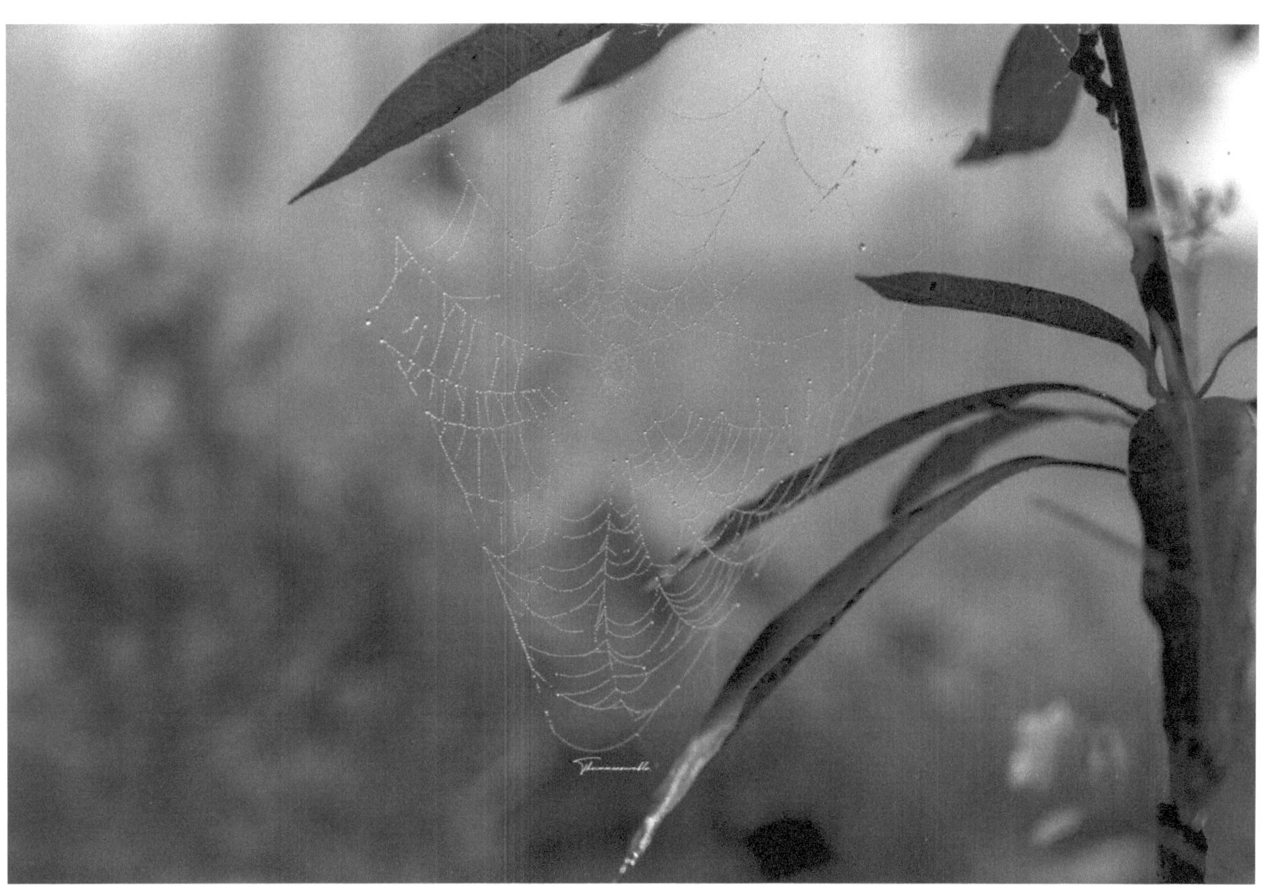

Surrendering the Pain

We hold suffering as if it defines us.
If only we allow ourselves to flow with the pain; we will find the answer in the centre of our being.
Not with force, but with grace.
Pain is not a prison—it is a passage.

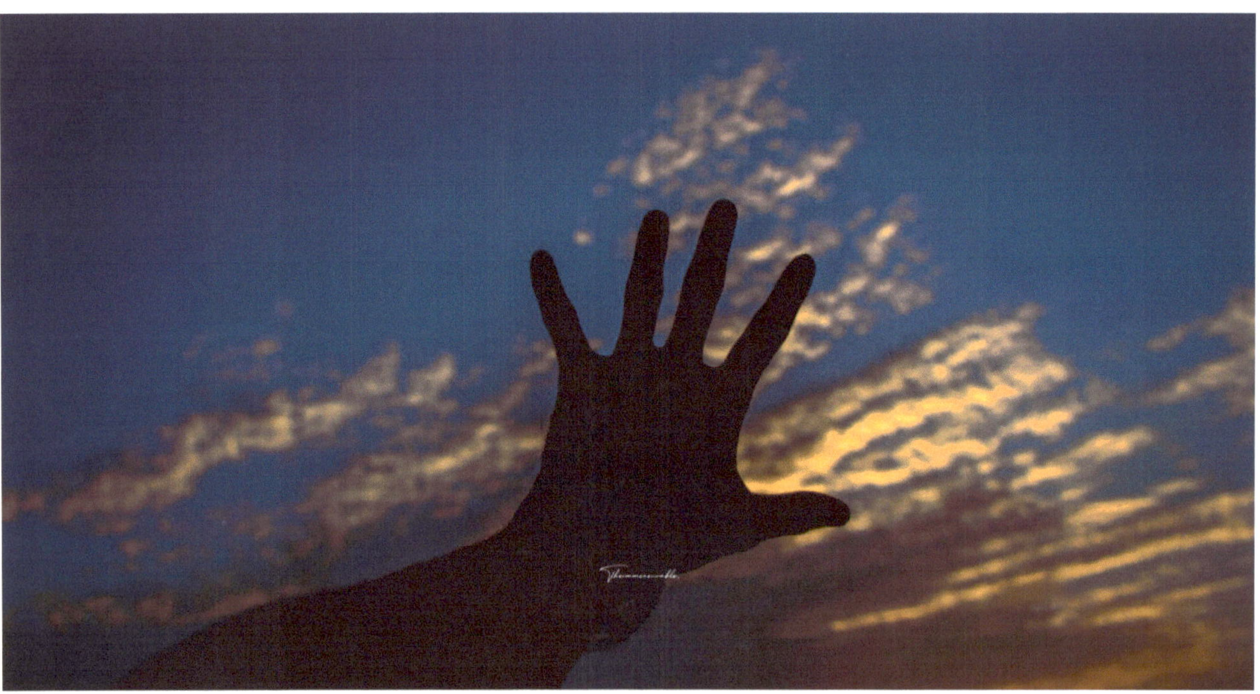

The Stillness That Saves

Stillness is where light begins. It begins not in seeking but in stopping.
Not in knowing, but in being.
Only then can you find a glimpse of "The Immeasurable."

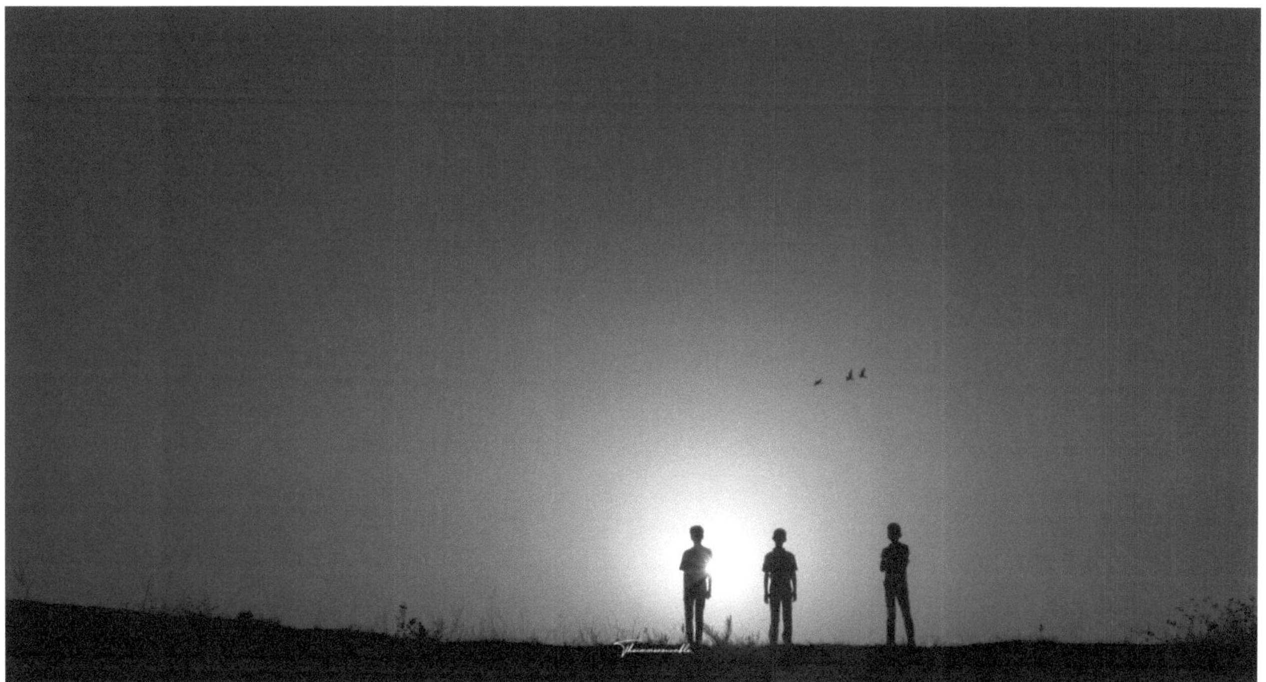

The Love That Awakens

See yourself. Then see others.
What you seek in another has always lived within you.
Separation is the grand illusion—love, the enormous truth.

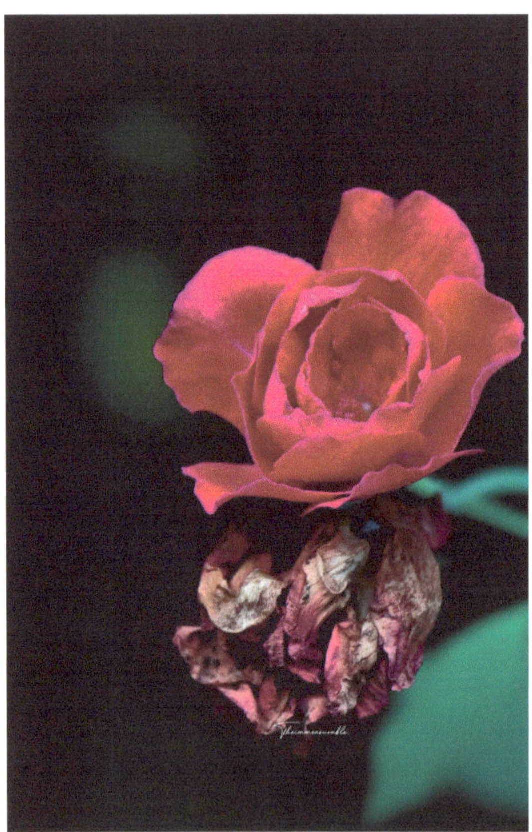

The Return to Light

The journey was never to escape the darkness.
It was to find that light was never missing— waiting to be seen.

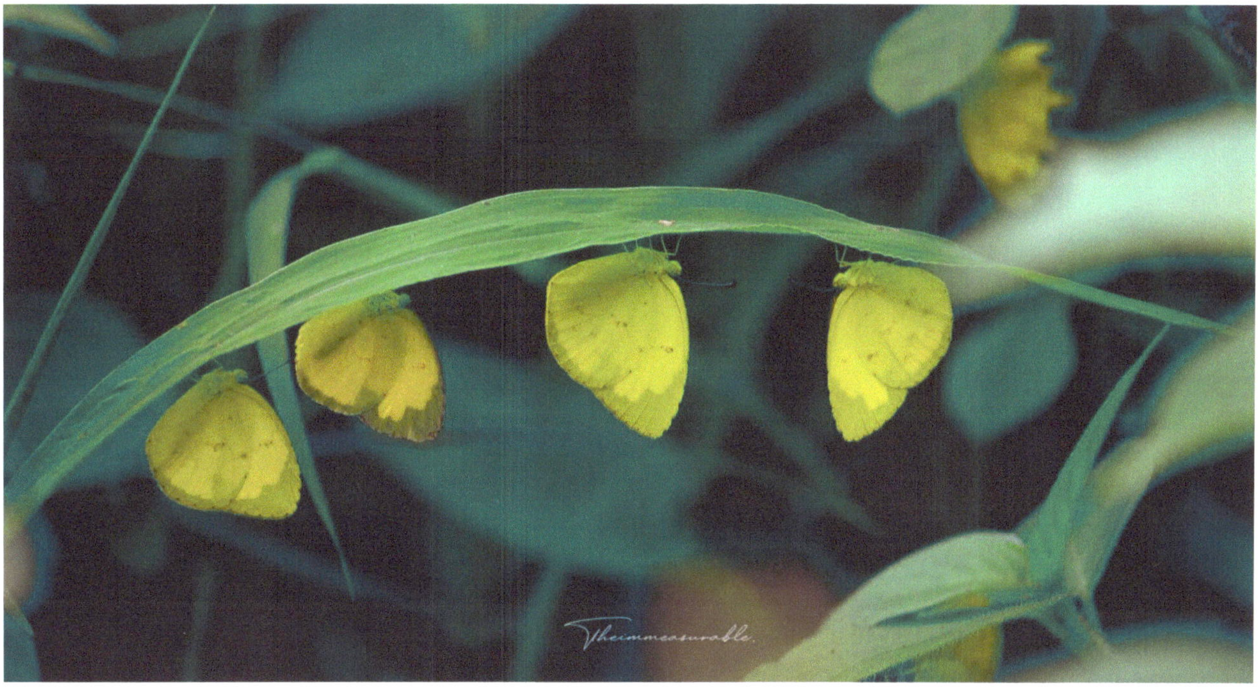

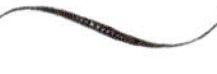

CHAPTER THREE

LIGHT WITHIN

Light Within

Was the light ever missing, or were your eyes closed?
What if the glow you sought—in stars, others, and fleeting moments—was already within you?
You walked through darkness. You faced the storm. Now, can you finally, see?

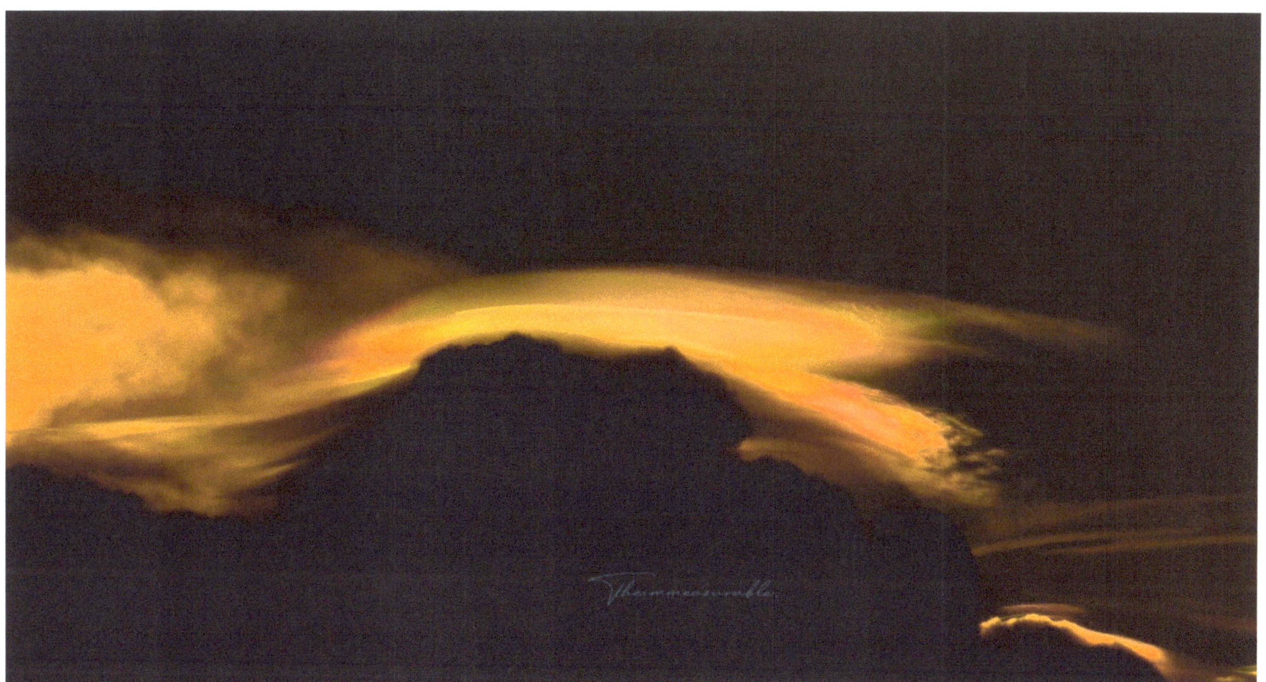

The Unveiling

Was it darkness or fear? What if darkness was never the enemy, but the stage where light reveals itself?
Close your eyes. Breathe. Feel it—the ember inside, waiting.
How long have you ignored your glow?

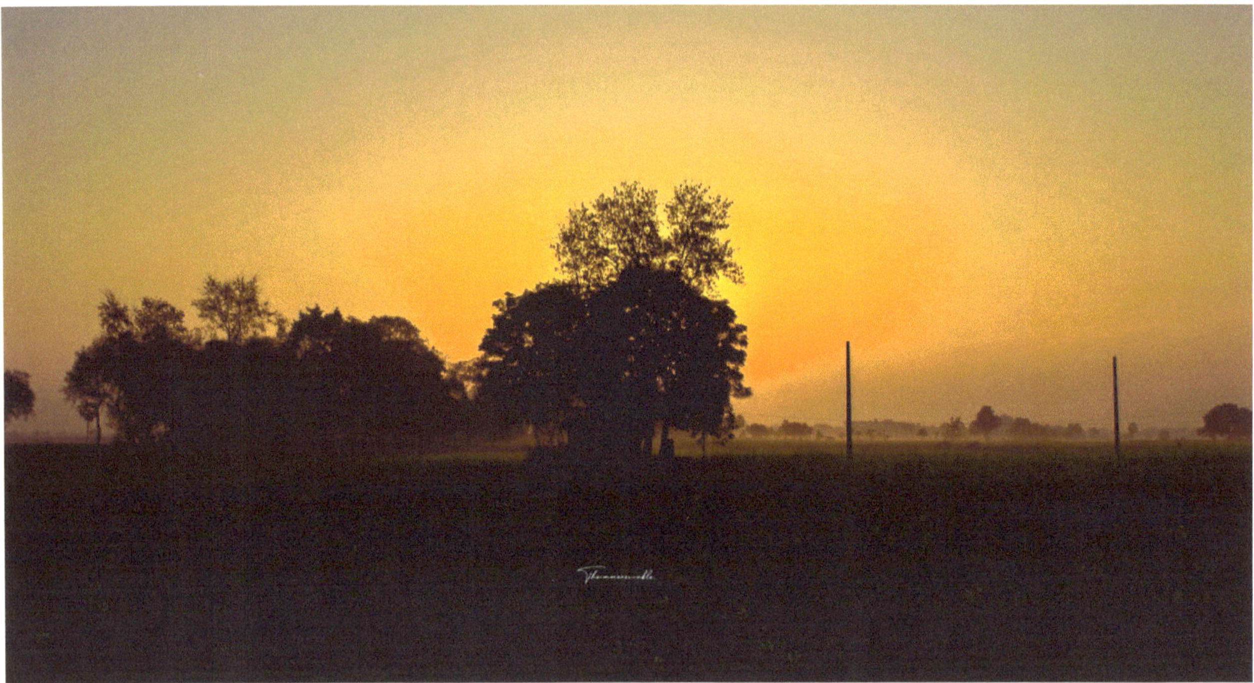

The First Glimmer

Do you remember when light first broke through?
Not a flash, but rather a whisper. A soft flicker in your being.
Did it come in silence? In surrender? In the pause between breaths, where does truth speak?

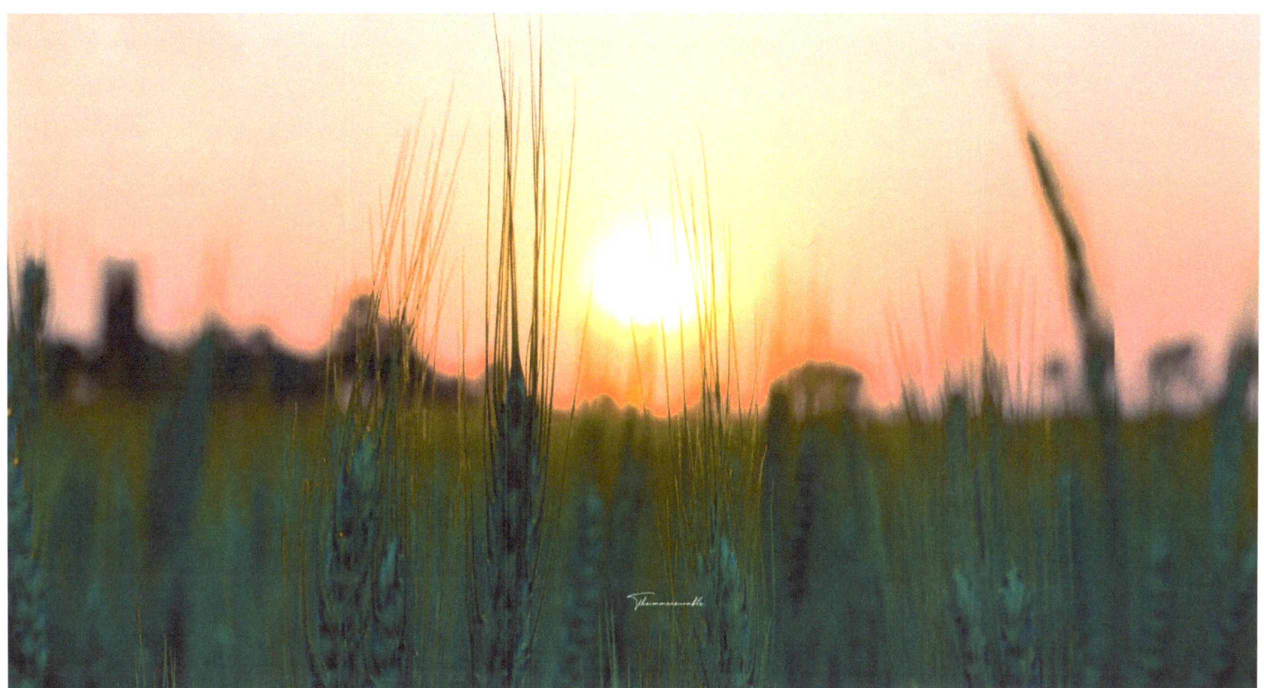

Becoming the Light

You are no longer searching. No longer reaching. You are remembering.
The journey was never about finding light—it was realizing you were the light all along.

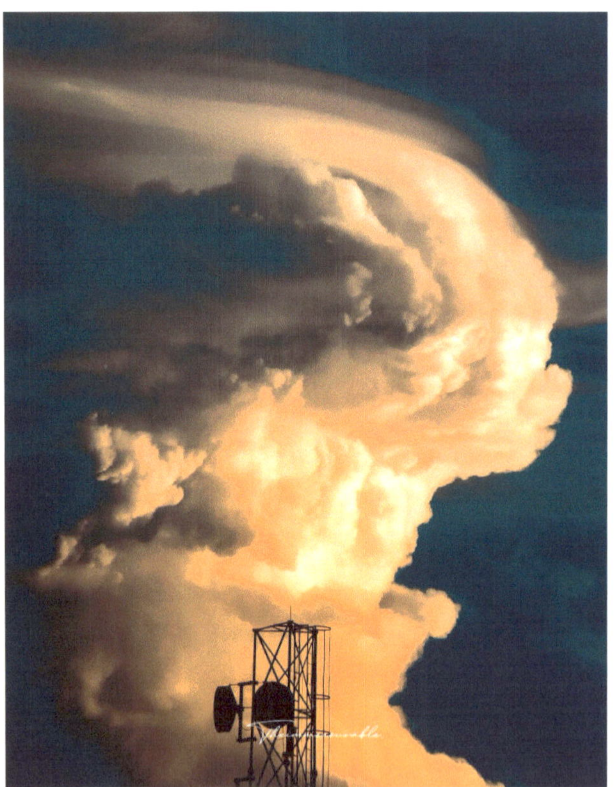

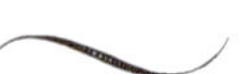

PEACE AND CALMNESS

Peace & Calmness

What happens when the search ends?
Is peace found, or does it emerge when you stop resisting?
You have walked through darkness. You have seen the light. Now, can you sit with it?

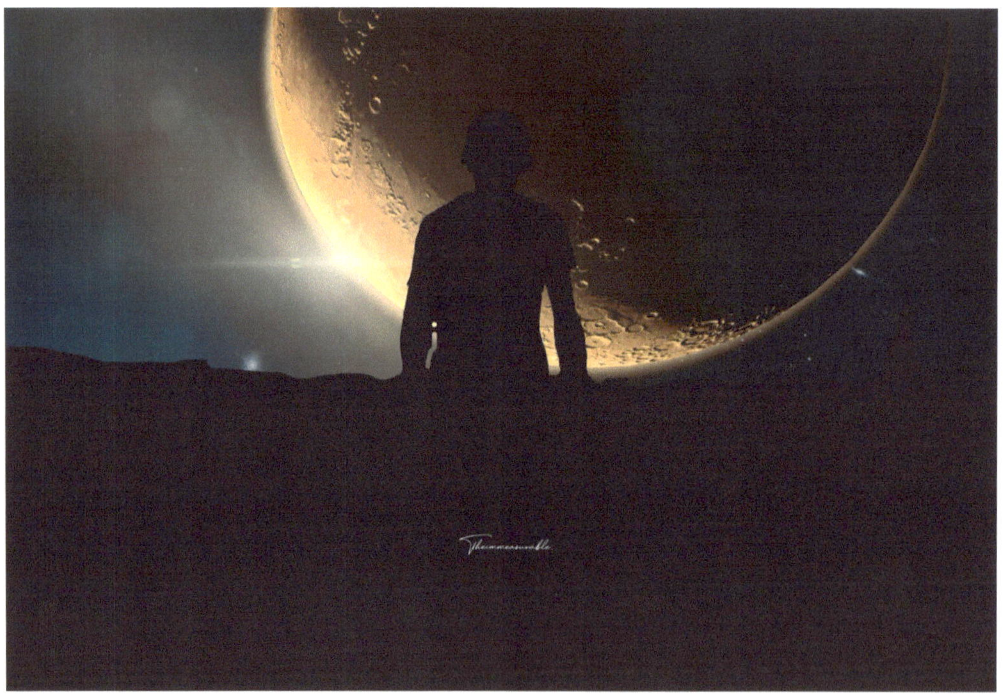

The Stillness Within

Like the ocean, wild on the surface yet calm in its depths—so is your soul. Peace isn't given; it's allowed. Not escape, not numbness, but presence.
Can you trust the flow instead of fighting the tide?

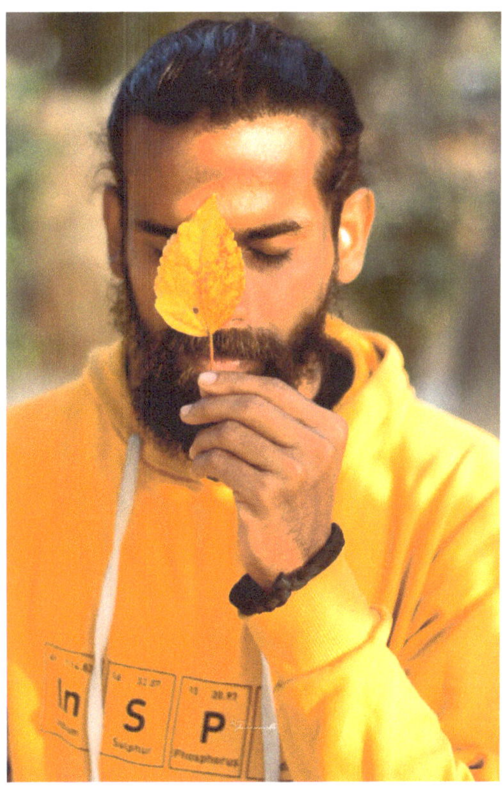

Beyond the Noise

Silence isn't emptiness—it's fullness.
You spent so long filling the void, but now you see: The void was always whole.
Peace isn't the lack of thought, but freedom from its grip.

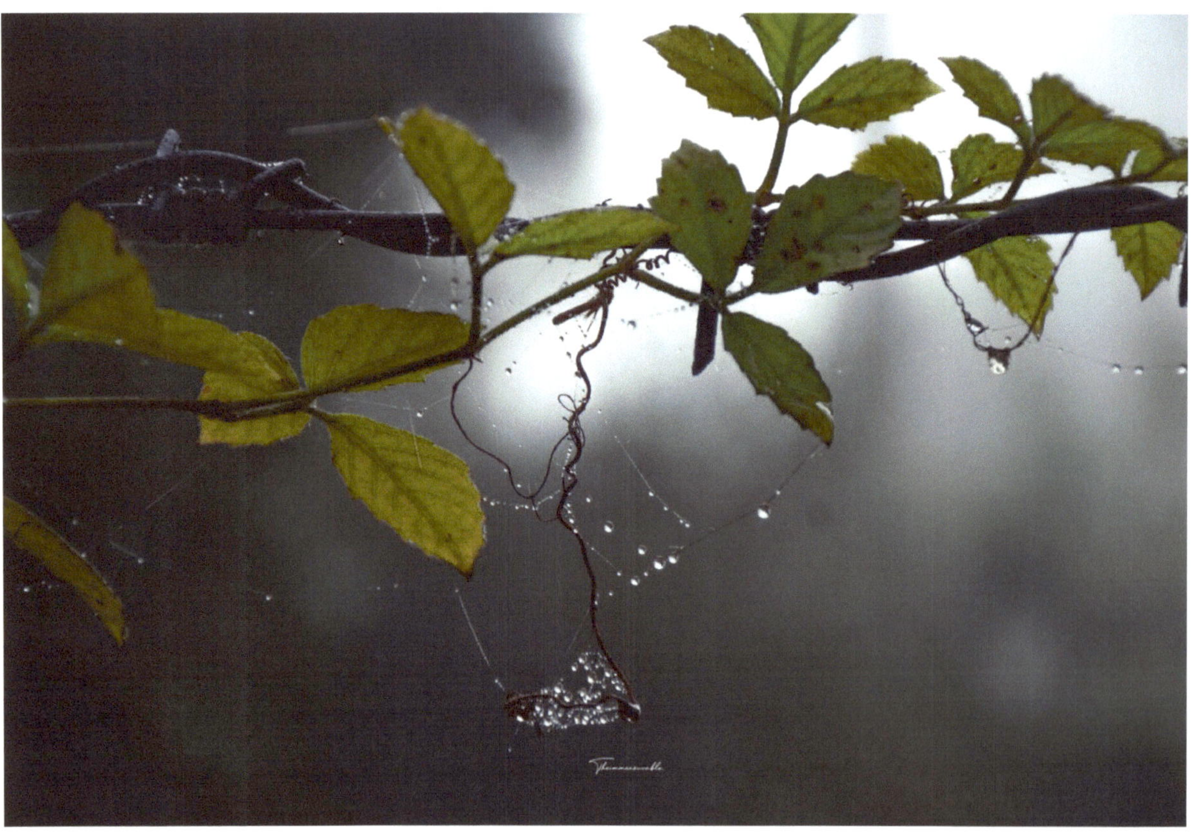

The Gentle Knowing

No more running.
No more grasping. You simply are.
The trees sway, rivers flow, stars burn—and you stand, unmoved. Unshaken. Home.

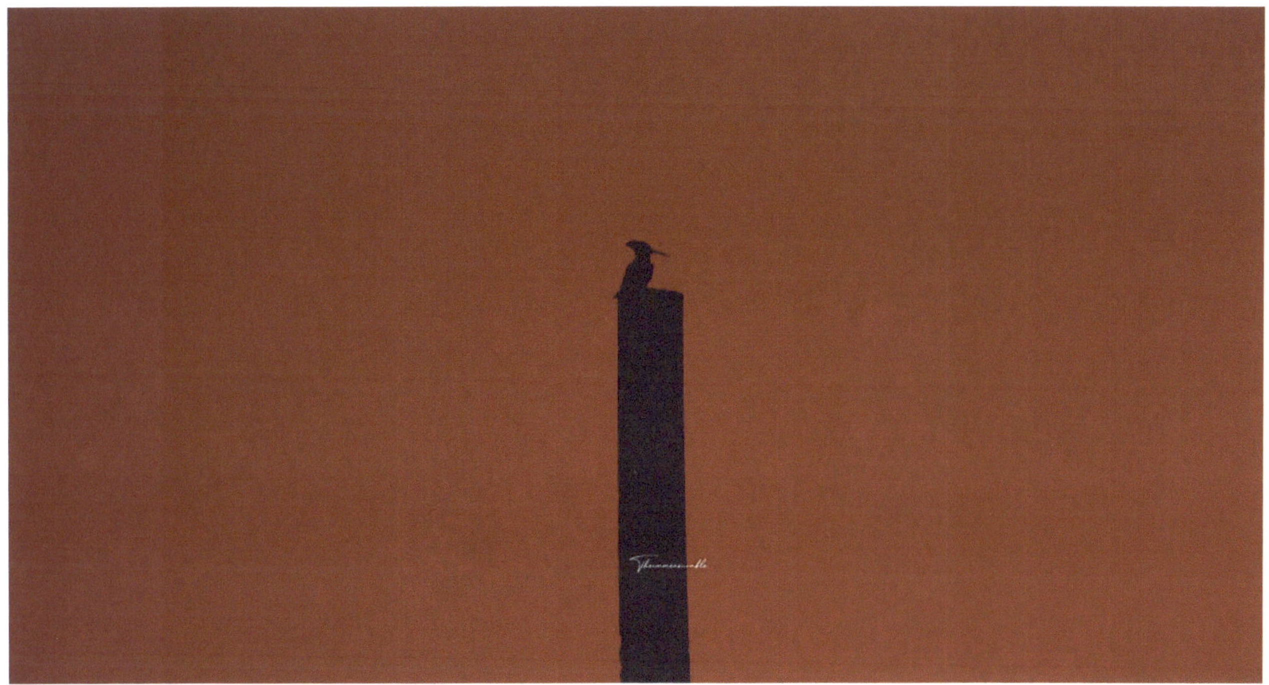

Deeper Understanding of Life

Do you know about life?

What if life is not a question to answer but an unfolding?
Have you ever stopped searching and simply observed—without thought, without judgment?
If truth has no road, is life not an endless discovery?

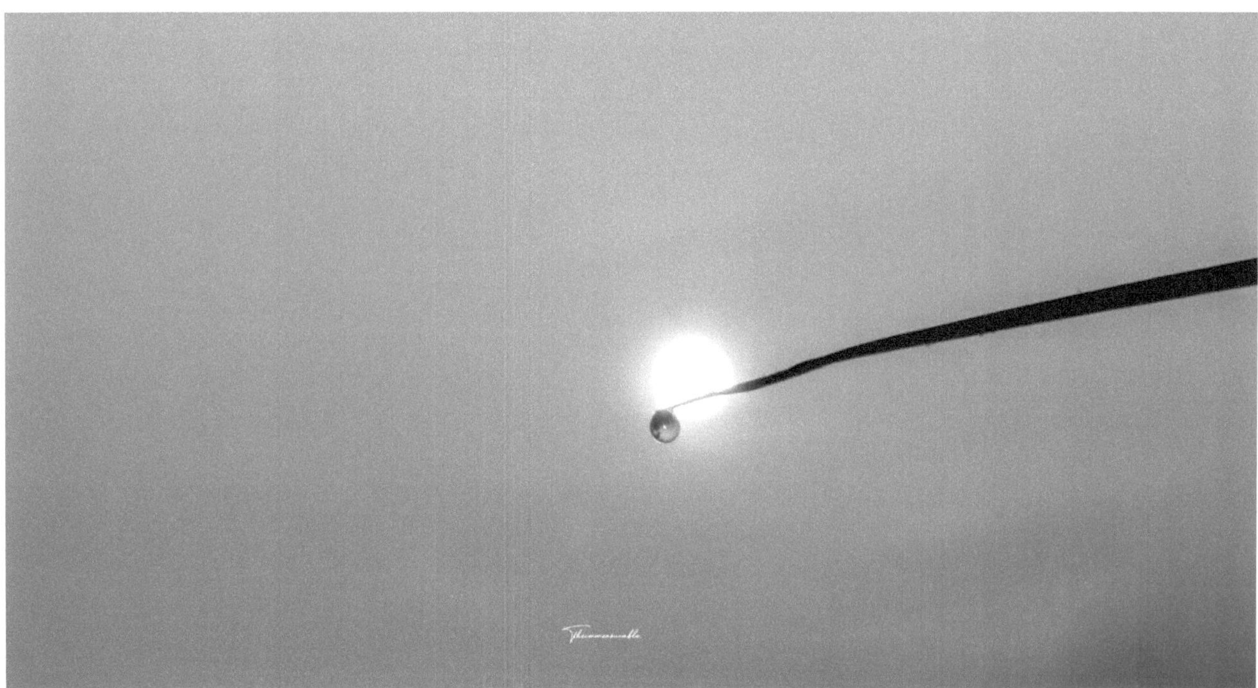

Seeing Clearly

Do you see life as it is or as you wish it to be?
How much of reality is shaped by memory, fear, and desire?
Drop labels. Drop judgments. See without attachment. What remains?

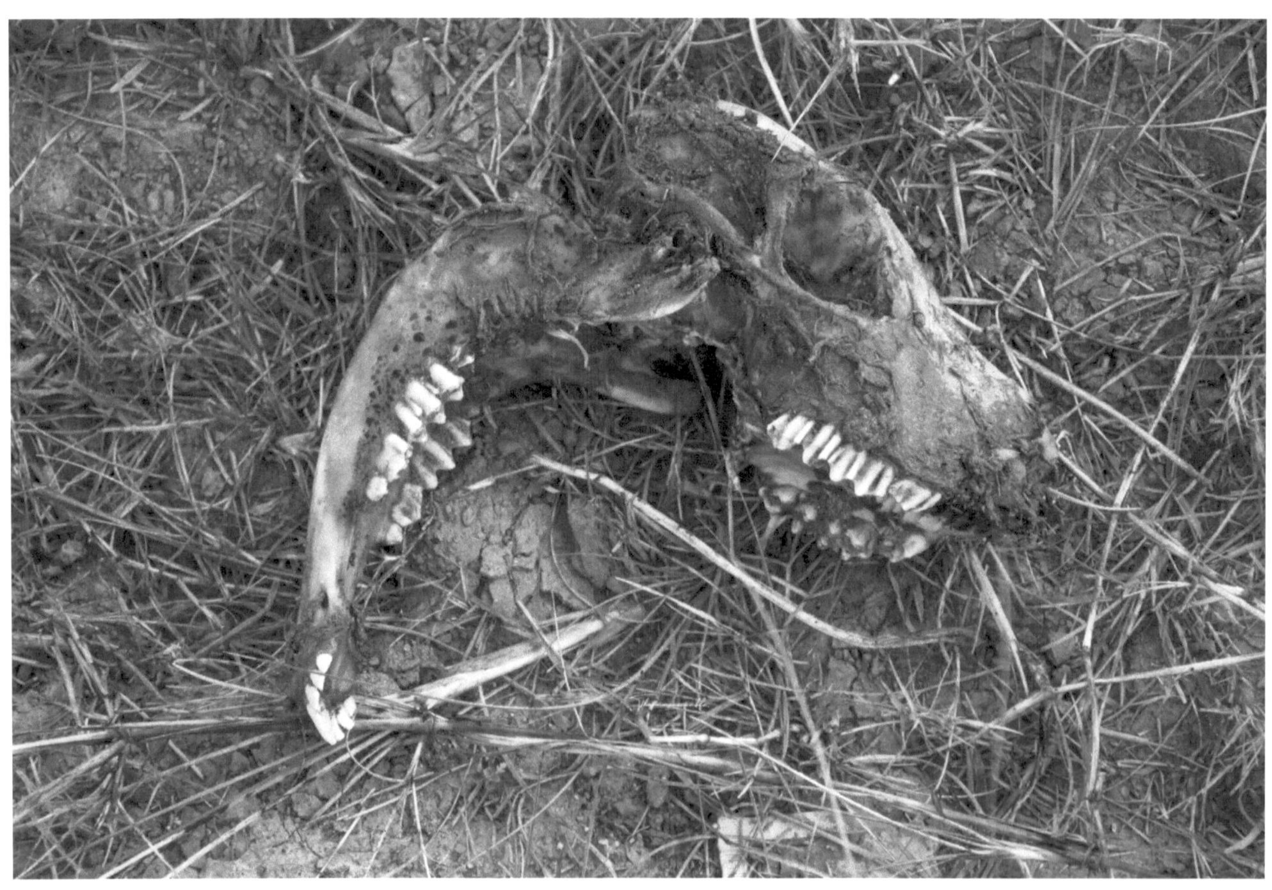

Letting Go of Control

Do you hold too tightly—to people, ideas, illusions?
Life flows, indifferent to your grasp. It does not wait for your permission to change.
Can you embrace it all—joy, sorrow, impermanence—without resistance?

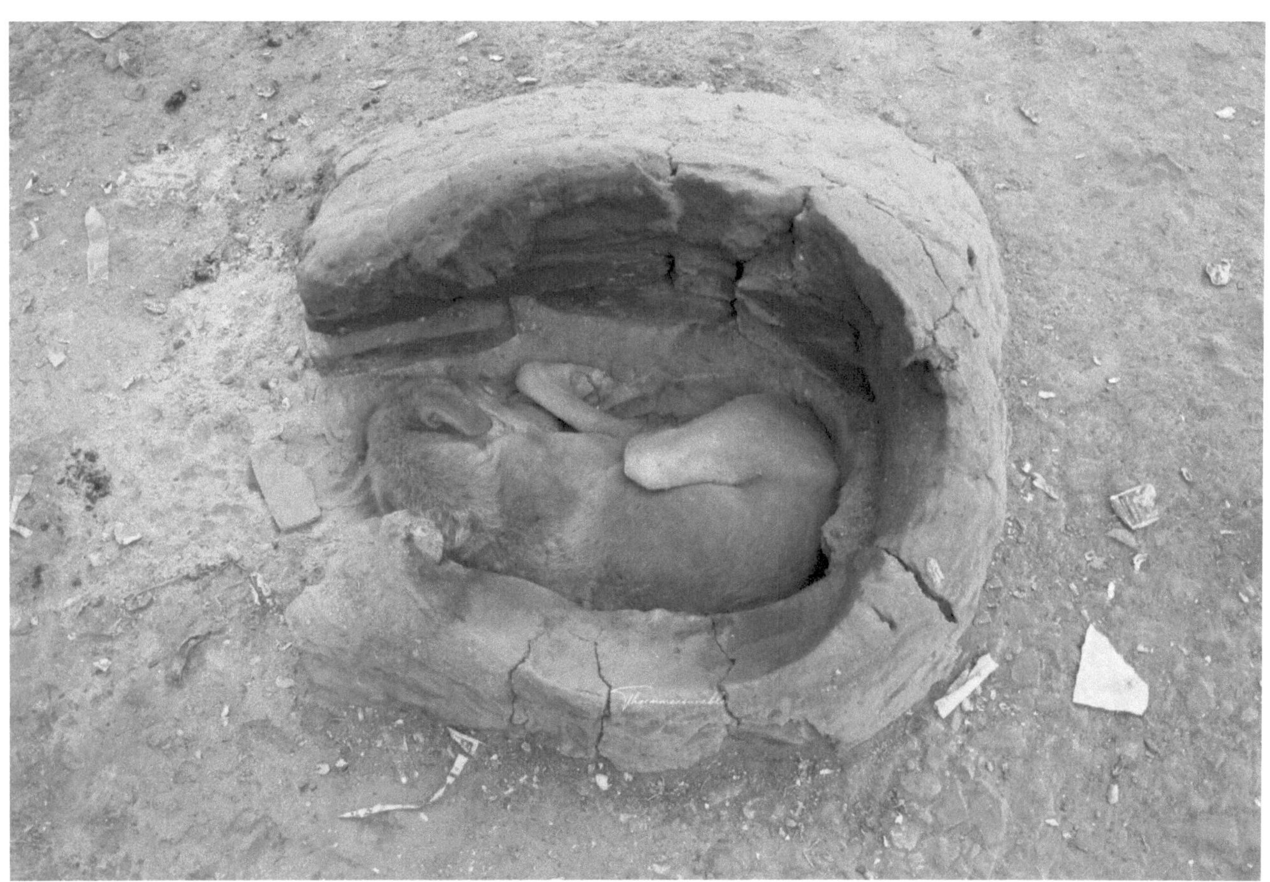

The Freedom of Impermanence

Everything you hold will one day be gone.
Does that frighten you or set you free? When you stop clinging, you start living.
When you stop searching, you start seeing. When you stop fearing, you start being.

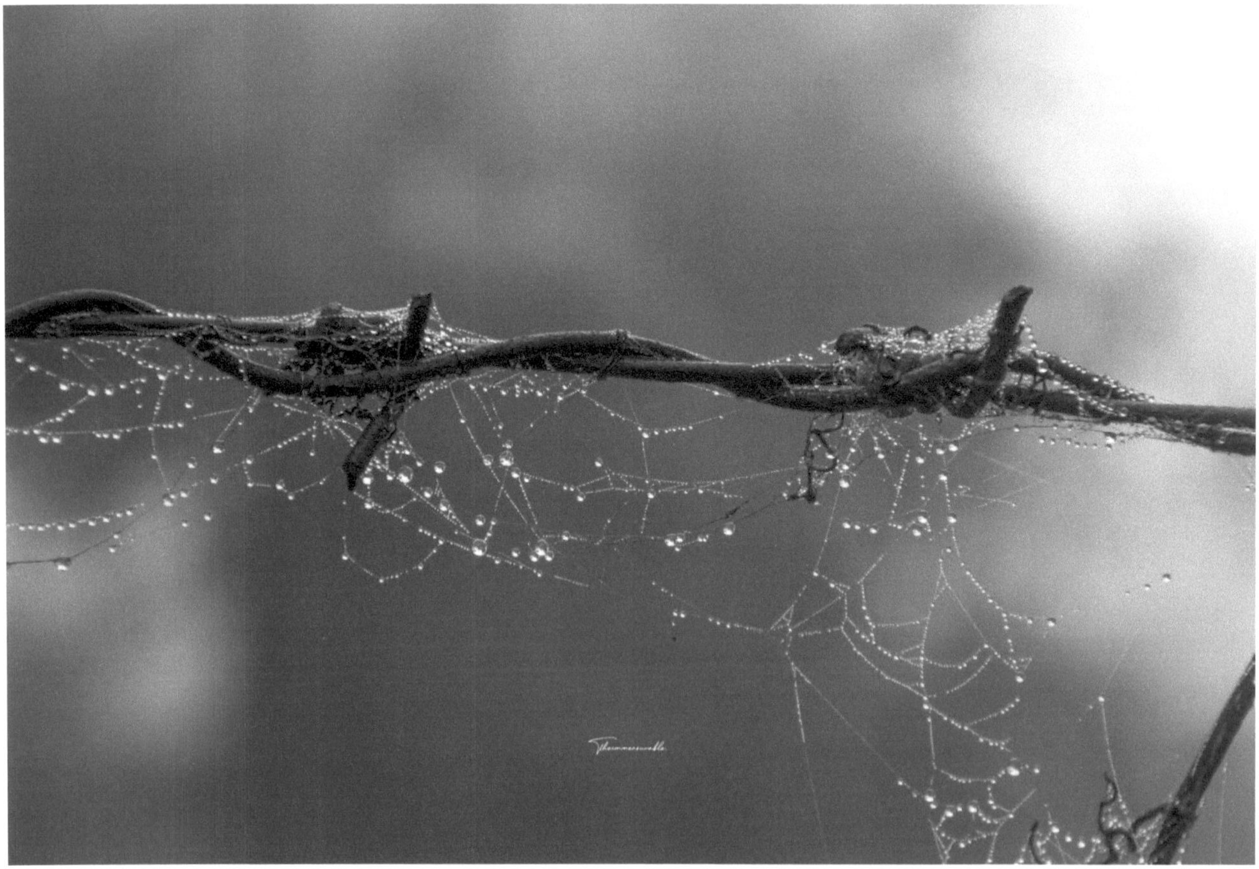

How "i Am Nothing" Got Its Name

The title "I Am Nothing" is not an absence but a presence—a surrender to the vastness of existence. It reflects a deep understanding that beyond identity, ego, and the constant search for meaning, there is a stillness, an openness, a space where true clarity emerges.

This book is a quiet rebellion in a world that urges us to define ourselves and chase titles and labels. It embraces the paradox: by becoming nothing, we become everything. By letting go of the need to be someone, we align with the boundless flow of life.

Each page of this photo book meditates on light and shadow, presence and impermanence, seeking and surrendering. It invites the reader to step beyond the self and be.

The title is not about emptiness but about freedom.

The freedom to exist without constraints, to see without distortion, and to embrace life as it unfolds—unfiltered, untamed, and infinite.

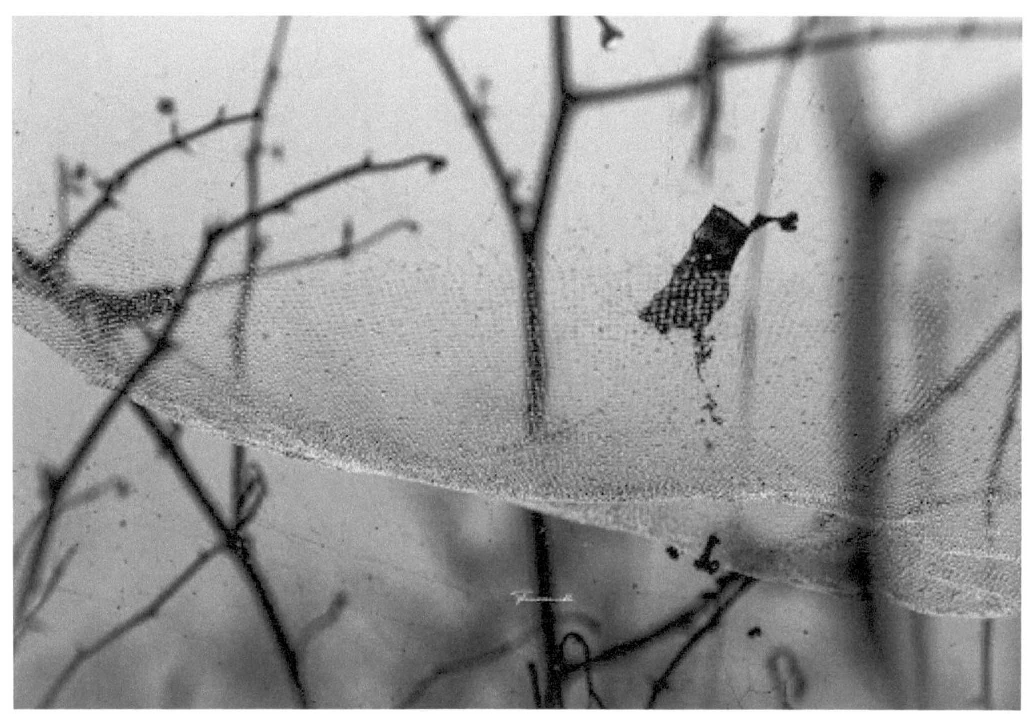

A Whisper To The Infinite

As these pages come to an end, the journey within continues. This book was never about finding answers but about remembering—the light, the stillness, the boundless presence that has always been.

To those who seek, to those who surrender, and to those who simply are—this work is for you.

We dedicate this book to The Immeasurable—the silent force that moves through all things, unseen yet ever present.

This is just the beginning. More journeys through self-discovery, captured in light and shadow, await in the future editions.

May you continue to see—not just with your eyes, but with your being.